T0062953

JOB HACK

The Quick & Easy-to-Use Guide to
Finding and Getting the Job You Want

CARISA MONTOOTH

BALBOA
PRESS

A DIVISION OF HAY HOUSE

Copyright © 2014 Carisa Montooth.

All rights reserved. No part of this book may be used or reproduced by any means, graphic, electronic, or mechanical, including photocopying, recording, taping or by any information storage retrieval system without the written permission of the publisher except in the case of brief quotations embodied in critical articles and reviews.

Balboa Press books may be ordered through booksellers or by contacting:

Balboa Press
A Division of Hay House
1663 Liberty Drive
Bloomington, IN 47403
www.balboapress.com
1 (877) 407-4847

Because of the dynamic nature of the Internet, any web addresses or links contained in this book may have changed since publication and may no longer be valid. The views expressed in this work are solely those of the author and do not necessarily reflect the views of the publisher, and the publisher hereby disclaims any responsibility for them.

The author of this book does not dispense medical advice or prescribe the use of any technique as a form of treatment for physical, emotional, or medical problems without the advice of a physician, either directly or indirectly. The intent of the author is only to offer information of a general nature to help you in your quest for emotional and spiritual well-being. In the event you use any of the information in this book for yourself, which is your constitutional right, the author and the publisher assume no responsibility for your actions.

Any people depicted in stock imagery provided by Thinkstock are models, and such images are being used for illustrative purposes only. Certain stock imagery © Thinkstock.

Printed in the United States of America.

ISBN: 978-1-4525-1831-2 (sc)
ISBN: 978-1-4525-1832-9 (e)

Balboa Press rev. date: 07/23/2014

CONTENTS

This book is dedicated to my lovely daughter, Cadence. May you find your life path at an early age and spend the rest of your life enjoying it. It's the joy of my life watching you become the person you came here to be.

ACKNOWLEDGEMENTS

To my wonderful husband, Sam, the most supportive person I have ever been blessed to know. Thanks for making me laugh whenever I feel like crying. Team Montooth!

To my parents, Marcia and C.J.—thank you for always being in my corner. I love you very much.

To my siblings—James, Regan, Bobby, and Allyson—thanks for being funny and smart. Keeping up with you all makes life interesting. Love ya.

To my best friend, Anna—thanks for believing in me and getting me to do things I don't think I'm ready for.

INTRODUCTION

Do you want to have a job that is satisfying for you, but you aren't sure how to figure out what kind of job will make you happy?

Do you need a quick, easy guide to the basic mechanics of a job search?

Do you want to be ready to walk in to an interview and feel confident about what to expect?

Do you need to have concise answers to your job search questions in a "quick and dirty" guide that gets to the point?

If you answered yes to any of these questions, then keep reading, because this short, easy-to-use guide is for you.

The book you hold in your hands will introduce you to the basics of figuring out what careers you are interested in, how to prepare for them, and how to get the job you want. Inside, you'll find links to lots of online sources of free career-related information, assessments, and resources.

Maybe you are reentering the workforce after an absence. You might already be employed and be thinking about changing careers. Perhaps you're a college student and you're wondering how much education and experience you will really need for the career you want. You could be a high school student about to graduate and wanting to know the basics of finding a job. Whatever your situation is, this short, easy-to-use guide will help you figure out what you need to do next and to do it.

As a college counselor, I spend a lot of time talking with students about careers—how to know which one is right for them, how to prepare for it once they've chosen a profession that interests them, how to find openings in the field, how to apply, and how to interview. This book is a short crash course in exactly that.

To give you some extra help in meeting your career goals, I've put together some special bonuses for you, absolutely free! You can access them at www.jobhackbook.com.

Best of luck to you in all of your career-related endeavors!

Carisa Montooth

Finding Out About You

I'm going to let you in on a secret.

Before you start looking for a career, it's important to figure out who you are. It's the single most important thing you can do to make sure you will be happy in your career down the road and get more joy out of your life. This concept seems simple, but people ignore it all the time and shortchange themselves. They end up less successful and less happy. It has to do with a really simple concept of identity versus role. Let me explain…

See, *your identity is who you are.* It's who you take with you all the time into any situation. It's your preferences and dislikes, your sense of humor, your hopes and dreams, and the essence of you.

Your *role*, on the other hand, is *what you do*. A role is being a student, a friend, a parent, or an employee. It's a tricky distinction, but it's very important to get it. When you choose roles that are a good fit for your identity, you are much, much happier. It's easier to be successful, and life is easier overall. When you choose roles that are in conflict with your identity, you are setting yourself up for stress and difficulty.

So, you can see why it's very important to figure out who you are. This sounds like a big question, right? All I really mean is that you need a clear idea of what your values are and what kinds of things interest you.

Once you know who you really are and what you like, you can choose a career that matches your values. For example, if helping people is important to you, you may be naturally interested in careers such as nursing, teaching, medicine, or activism. Once you have an idea of the values that are important to you (e.g., helping people, working outdoors, solving problems, etc.), you know which direction to head in. Then you can narrow down your interests within that particular field.

You may not have had the chance to give your values some serious thought before. That's okay. That's just part of the overall process of becoming the person you want to be. We are all working toward becoming better versions of ourselves. Taking the time to figure out your values will help you in your career and, even more importantly, it will help you in *every other area of your life.*

As an extra bonus for you, I've put together some free resources you can access online that will help you in different areas of your journey. Come check them out at www.jobhackbook.com. So let's get started…

Why You Should Choose Your Job Instead of Letting It Choose You

If you ask people why they are in the field that they are in, many of them will tell you that they chose their job out of necessity. Often when people are in a difficult situation financially or just need to start making money as quickly as possible, they will choose jobs based on availability rather than choose professions that are in line with their values and interests. If it sounds like I'm describing your situation, don't worry. I'm going to show you some ways to get back on track, beginning with personality and career assessments.

Sometimes my students will ask, "What about just getting a job right now to make money and then just switching to something I like better later?" A problem people in this situation encounter is that once they've invested a lot of time and energy into rising through the ranks in a profession, they are *very reluctant* to change direction, even when they are extremely unhappy in their current job. They feel they've invested so much in that job that it would be unwise to seek out something different. It's the exact same mentality of people who invest in a stock and then refuse to sell it once it goes bad. They keep the stock because they've invested so much money in it and they hope that if they keep it longer, it will go up in value.

As you become more skillful and experienced working in a job, you will probably find that you are still able to receive promotions and rise through the ranks, even if you don't particularly care for the job. However, you eventually find yourself midway up a ladder that you didn't really choose to climb. This can be a very difficult situation to be in. You can find that you do not take much pleasure in performing your job duties. After the excitement of the additional money that comes with a promotion wears off, a job that you don't really like is still a job that you don't really like.

If you are making good money but you hate your job, you can't really be happy. Usually you back yourself into a corner, because the money supports a lifestyle you would like to enjoy, but you can't actually enjoy it because you hate what you do. It's a "catch-22."

Another reason people sometimes stay in jobs they dislike is that they don't want to disappoint people in their lives. Sometimes, the people in our lives are very invested in our staying the same as we have always been. When they see us change direction in a career or in life, it can be scary for them. They may try to discourage you for reasons that actually have nothing to do with you. This situation is very common. Incidentally, if you find yourself in this circumstance, think about it this way—if you need advice about how to go in a new direction successfully, whom should you take it from? People who are stuck and want you to stay stuck, or people who have successfully moved forward in their lives? Take it from other people who have changed directions successfully in their own careers and in their own lives. In fact, the following is a good rule of thumb. *Anytime you need advice about how to do something successfully in your career or in any other area of your life, take it from the people who are already doing the thing you want to be doing—and who are doing it well.*

But let's return to your current job situation. You may be saying, "I need to keep my job even if I hate it, because I need the money." Ask yourself honestly, though, if you really believed that you didn't have any other option but to keep a job you hate, would you have started reading this book? Nope.

You have unique gifts and strengths. There are things you want to do and things you are naturally good at. Somewhere, someone wants to pay you to do those things. Money is important and necessary, but so is doing something with your life that resonates with you, fulfills you, and makes you feel proud to talk about what you do. Investing a bit of time and energy in learning about yourself and the job search process can help you start on a path to a career that you really, really like… maybe even love.

Do you know how people tell you that you should "do what you love, and the money will come"? *Well, it's absolutely true, and I'll tell you why.* When you love what you do, you devote more time to it than people who aren't as passionate about it, and you eventually become an expert at it. You eat, sleep, and breathe it. You want to talk about it all the time. You buy books about it, go to conferences about it, and post Facebook comments about it. People can tell that you know your stuff. People can see that you *love* what you are doing, because they can see how passionate you are about it and what an expert you are. In a field of competitors, *you will stand out.*

So let's move on to the business of learning more about yourself and discovering what you are passionate about.

Figuring Out Who You Are

There are lots of different ways to learn more about yourself. One of the easiest ways to do this is to use a career assessment. Don't let the name fool you—career assessments aren't only for choosing careers. Career assessments, interest inventories, and personality inventories are really just ways of getting very clear feedback about what things are important to you.

Assessments and inventories can give you very valuable information, but remember, they aren't the only ways to get clear about what your strengths and values are. Think about qualities that others have told you repeatedly you have had since you were a kid or the kinds of qualities you frequently receive compliments for now. When I was a kid, I wanted to make new kids in my class feel welcome. My elementary school counselor noticed this and asked me to be a part of the Friendship Club. When I came home from school, I would say hello to every neighbor in every apartment all the way up the courtyard on the way to my apartment. Today, I'm a counselor, which means that I get to help people for a living. What about you? Did you have a lemonade stand every summer? Maybe you have the makings of an entrepreneur. Did you show an early talent for music? You could pursue a career as a musician. Do you love playing video games? You could become a game designer, programmer, or animator. There is always some little inkling of your strengths and gifts from an early age, so don't discount those stories from your parents or teachers that show the early evidence of your gifts and talents.

But let's talk about career assessments. There are many different types of career assessments, but here are a few:

- **Strongest Element Personality Framework:** The Strongest Element Personality Framework is a fun, quick, and easy system that I have developed to help people understand personality differences. Each of the four main personality types is represented by an element of nature—earth, air, water, or fire. When you take the Strongest Element Personality Framework test, it will show you which is your "strongest element," or dominant personality type. The profiles of the personality types are condensed down from the sixteen personality types you will find in the Myers Briggs Temperament Inventory (see below) and based on the work of Carl Jung. If you would like to take the Strongest Element Personality Framework test, you can do so on my website, www.carisamontooth.com. I would love to work with you personally (yes, you!) to help you figure out which personality type you are and what careers might match that.

- **Eureka Skills Inventories**: The Eureka website (www.eureka.org) is a great resource for career self-assessments. Their website is helpful for determining which characteristics describe you, which careers fit those characteristics, and which resources you can use to prepare for those careers.

- **Myers Briggs Temperament Inventory**: The Myers Briggs Temperament Inventory, or MBTI (see www.myersbriggs.org for a more detailed description) is an instrument that can give you a very thorough understanding of your temperament (i.e., personality). When your answers on the MBTI are interpreted, you receive a four-digit code that tells you if you are

- Introverted (I) or extroverted (E): Do you prefer to focus on the outer world or on your own inner world?
- Sensing (S) or intuitive (N): Do you prefer to focus on the basic information you take in, or do you prefer to interpret and add meaning?
- Thinking (T) or feeling (F): When making decisions, do you prefer to first look at logic and consistency or to first look at the people and special circumstances?
- Judging (J) or perceiving (P): In dealing with the outside world, do you prefer to get things decided or do you prefer to stay open to new information and options?

- **Holland Occupational Themes (also known as the RIASEC inventory):** The RIASEC inventory was developed by psychologist John Holland in the late 1950s. Each letter corresponds to a particular value that is dominant in a personality type: R = realistic, I = investigative, A = artistic, S = social, E = enterprising, and C = conventional. Each of these personality types is drawn to a particular set of occupations. You can take this assessment at http://www.cacareerzone. org/quick.

Finding Out About Careers

Now that you understand yourself better and have a clearer picture of your preferences, values, strengths and talents, it's time to learn what's out there career-wise that would match you well.

Career Exploration Classes

Taking a career exploration class is a great way to learn which careers match your values. If you have the time to take a career exploration class, it would definitely be worth your while. If you'd like to take a class, look at the class schedules at nearby community colleges. An additional advantage to taking a career course at a community college is that many community colleges offer college credit for career exploration courses. If your career requires you to get a college degree, you can use these credits from your course toward your degree. Some of these courses are offered online as well as in person.

When you take a career exploration course at a community college, your instructor will usually be a counselor. If you need help discovering your career and finding a path to it, community college counselors are very valuable resources. Taking a class allows you to work with a counselor who can help with career advice that is specific to your personality, values, and goals. Most counselors take a personal interest in their students, especially when they can see how interested the student is in making educated choices about his or her future. After all, that is really what we counselors are there for! We're there to give you the information that you need so that you can make a wise and educated choice that helps you build a satisfying future for yourself.

As a part of your career exploration course, you will usually visit the college's career library or career resource center. You will have access to information in the form of career guides, college guides, online career assessments, and other resources. You would usually take a career assessment in a career exploration class and receive a printout of a list of careers that align with your interests and personality. There it is: your list of jobs that you would be good at! Think of it as a jumping-off point to start your research.

Local businesses advertise their job openings through many college resource centers. In addition, you can often find postings about workshops on topics that might be useful to you, like writing resumes or doing well in interviews.

One of the greatest features you will find in a well-stocked career library is the reference books that give you information about the day-to-day activities of people in the field you want to go into. A lot of people don't realize that the job they are learning about in school will be a completely different thing when they are actually doing it every day. This is why internships are so valuable. They can help you learn what the real, day-to-day responsibilities of your job would be. (Skip to the section on internships if you want more information about that.)

If you don't have the time to take a class in person or you'd just rather get your information online, skip ahead to the section on online career research. In that section, I'll give you some websites that will help you get the information that you need online—and in most cases, it's free.

Career Workshops and Career Fairs

If you aren't able to invest the time in a career exploration course, you can find a career exploration workshop. These workshops typically require a time commitment of one morning or afternoon. You will find them at a nearby college or community center.

When you sign up for a career workshop, you will have the opportunity to work on your resume with a career development professional. Often they have good tips about how to present yourself in the best possible light with your resume. You may be worried that you don't have enough experience to add to your resume to make it worthwhile, or you may wonder how to show the parts of your experience that would be relevant to a new job. A career workshop is an ideal place to bring these concerns, because the workshop facilitator can give you advice that is much more specific to your situation than what you would normally receive from a career guidance book or online source.

Career fairs are another useful resource. Colleges host career fairs so that local employers have an opportunity to connect to students who are almost ready to graduate. If you are a college student at a college that hosts career fairs, it is definitely worth your time to check one out (even if it's on a day you wouldn't normally be on campus). I know of many students who received job offers through career fairs before they had even completed their degrees! Once they were done, they had jobs to go to right out of college in fields they were interested in and well prepared for.

Online Career Research

First off, let me say that I do not endorse any specific websites. That being said, there are a few that I use frequently and that I have found to be very helpful. If you don't have time to take a career guidance course in person or you are just taking a few baby steps toward figuring out your career path (or new career path), some of these resources may be helpful for you.

- **California Career Zone:** California Career Zone (www. cacareerzone.org) offers tools to help you assess your personality traits and learn about career options. They also offer a tool that gives you a "reality check" by helping you determine what your living expenses will be after high school and which occupations will pay that much. The information provided on the California Career Zone website can be accessed for free.
- **The Occupational Outlook Handbook (OOH):** The OOH is published each year by the U.S. Bureau of Labor Statistics (www.bls.gov). It describes important characteristics of different occupations. The OOH helps you answer questions about a career, like

  - What exactly do people in this field do?
  - How much does it pay on average?
  - What type of education is required for entry-level positions in this field?
  - Is this a field that is growing?

  You can access the information on the Bureau of Labor Statistics website at no charge, unless you want to buy a specific publication. To find the OOH online, go to www.bls. gov and click on "Publications."
- **My Next Move:** My Next Move (www.mynextmove.org) is an easy-to-use website that lets you find information about careers by doing a keyword search and browsing for specific careers by looking at the larger industry the career is a part of. If you have no idea where to begin, you can click on "Tell

us what you like to do." That takes you to the "O*Net Interest Profiler," which asks questions about your interests and then matches you with careers that fit these interests. You can also search categories like "Registered Apprenticeship,"", "Job Prep," and "Green" (i.e., careers in the green economy). *If you are a military veteran looking for work*, you can go to My Next Move for Veterans at www.mynextmove.org/vets/. My Next Move is created by the Education and Training Administration of the Department of Labor. The information is provided on the website at no charge.

- **Lynda.com:** If you don't mind paying a twenty-five-dollar monthly fee, you could check out www.lynda.com. Lynda. com offers online tutorials on job search–related subjects like writing resumes, as well as online tutorials about improving your skills (e.g., social media marketing, data analysis, etc.). You can take classes online to learn how to use different parts of the Microsoft Office suite (e.g. Word, PowerPoint, Excel, Access), which would be helpful for you to know for any type of a clerical support position. If you need to learn how to use design software, you can go to Lynda.com for help with SketchBook Pro and Adobe Illustrator. You can learn how to use CAD software or improve your knowledge of programmer software like Ruby, Python, or Java. You can browse the library for free to see if courses are offered that would be useful for you, before making a decision about signing up for a membership.

Informational Interviews

Interviewing people who are already working in the field you want to work in is the best way to find out what it's really like to have the career you want to have. All of the research you do will be very helpful, but it won't answer all of your questions.

How will you find someone to interview? There are a few different things you can do:

- **You can join professional organizations**. Many of these offer student memberships at a discounted price. Professional organizations usually host annual events that members can attend. These events are great for getting to know other people in the field you are interested in. In addition to finding people who are willing to share their experiences in the field with you, you can develop relationships that can lead to fantastic opportunities in the future.
- **You can contact college instructors who teach in the field you are interested in**. If you share a genuine interest in a field with an instructor, you will find that most are happy to help you learn more about it, especially if you are enrolled in the instructor's class.
- **You can approach someone in the field directly**. If you know someone who is already doing the job you want, see if he or she will let you ask a few questions about it. Most people would be flattered if you respectfully share an interest in their work and would be willing to discuss it with you.

It is vital that you choose the person you are going to interview as carefully as possible. You want to choose someone who is successful at what he or she is doing or who has specific qualities that you would like to emulate. Sometimes it is difficult to discover whether a person fulfills these criteria before you meet with him or her for the interview, or you may have limited choices of people that you can ask to interview. In any case, pay attention to a few things:

- Pay attention to the way that others around you interact with the person you are interviewing. Do they treat that person with respect? Are they surprised to find that someone would want to interview the person you are interviewing? These are important clues to understanding how the person you are getting information from is regarded in his or her field or office.

- If people you are talking with don't seem to understand much about what you are asking them, they might not be the best people to talk with. Don't bail out on the interview, though! If you are polite and tactful, they may be able to refer you to someone else who can be more helpful.

- Take the behavior of the people you are interviewing with a grain of salt. If they are rude to you, don't take it personally. While I was in college, I interviewed an elementary school counselor to get some insight into her day-to-day experiences in order to make an informed choice about whether I wanted to work in elementary schools or in colleges. Out of consideration for her time, I checked with her in advance to see if she would be interested in speaking with me and to see if she had time. Although she did have time and said she was interested in speaking with me, she behaved very strangely throughout our entire interview. I learned later that she suspected I was interested in either taking her job or reporting some kind of misbehavior on her part, neither of which was true. I was totally astounded to learn of her concern; I didn't even have a counseling degree yet! The moral of the story is, do what you can to put people at ease, but don't take any strange behavior you encounter personally.

What will you ask them? Spend some time thinking about exactly what you would like to know about the field and come prepared with a few specific questions.

For example, you may want to ask

- How did you prepare for this career (e.g., education, experience, skills, etc.)?
- What do you enjoy the most about this career?

- What is the most challenging part of this career? How do you overcome that?
- How are the day-to-day activities of this career different than you imagined they would be?*
- What advice would you give someone coming in to this field?*

*These are the most important questions you could possibly ask. They can save you lots of time and heartache. Learn from someone else's experiences whenever you can, rather than having to make all of your own mistakes.

Things to Think About

- **Be professional.** Dress appropriately. (See the section on interviewing for some ideas about dressing appropriately.)
- **Respect their time**. Be on time, and ask well-thought-out questions. Show your enthusiasm. Make eye contact with them when they speak to you. Ask them to explain things you don't understand the first time so that you can understand them fully.
- **Be willing to reciprocate**. If you are friendly and respectful, most people are happy to share some of their time or knowledge without expecting something in return. However, your thoughtfulness is appreciated and remembered. You don't have to do anything huge or beyond your means. Consider interviewing them over coffee, your treat. Always send a short thank you note or e-mail.

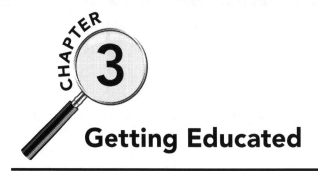

Getting Educated

Getting Educated

We've been covering the importance of choosing your career based on the best match for your personality type. While this is very important to consider, it is also important to think about how much time you are willing and able to invest in *educating yourself* to prepare for your career.

Some careers require a considerable investment of time and resources. For example, many doctoral programs (programs that provide you with a doctorate degree, like a PhD, PsyD, JD, or MD) involve a commitment of seven to eight years of postsecondary education and an internship of some kind. This type of an educational commitment can prevent you from being able to make a living while you are going to school, unless you can find a program that is specifically geared toward working professionals.

If you are interested in picking up some specific job skills without actually completing an entire degree or certificate program, you may be interested in sites like Lynda.com. At Lynda.com you can find information about job search skills (e.g. resume writing, cover letters, etc.) and you can also learn specific job skills from short, online tutorials about topics like animation, email marketing, management, architecture and accounting to name a few. Although there is a $25 monthly membership fee, you can browse the library of courses offered first to see if the investment is worthwhile for you. It is much cheaper than a college course and may be the extra boost of education you need that gets you the job you want.

Different careers require different levels of educational preparation.

When you are considering investing your time, money, and energy into an educational program, it is a wise idea to check on the reputation of the program. One way of checking on the reputation of a program would be to check on its accreditation. Accreditation is a measure of accountability for a school; when a school is accredited, this means that the school has agreed to be held to high standards of accountability and that it will be critiqued regularly to confirm that it is continuing to meet those standards. The Western Association of Schools and Colleges (WASC) is responsible for accrediting senior (four-year) colleges in the western United States. You can find information about schools they have accredited online at www. wascsenior.org. You can also research accreditation for junior colleges through the Accrediting Commission for Community and Junior Colleges (ACCJC), which is a subdivision of WASC, at www.accjc.org.

Vocational Education

Vocational education is specific to an occupation or a craft. Vocational education is sometimes referred to as "technical education," due to its focus on mastering the performance of specific technical skills. Vocational programs are offered through a vocational school (e.g., DeVry) or a community college. The time commitment for these programs is generally two years or less, depending on the program. Vocational programs focus on preparing you to begin working in your chosen field right away. When you complete a vocational program, you receive a certificate rather than a degree.

Some of the careers that a vocational education will prepare you for are as follows:

- Mechanic
- Police officer
- Child-care worker
- Interior designer
- Truck driver
- Photographer
- Legal assistant
- Embalmer
- Receptionist
- Dental hygienist
- Air traffic controller
- Real estate agent
- Tour guide
- Salesperson
- Flight attendant
- Travel agent

As you can see from the list above, there are interesting, well-paying careers that a vocational education could prepare you for. Look into vocational programs at your local community colleges to see what programs are available near you. Not every college offers every vocational program, so you need to check the schools in your area to find a particular program you are interested in.

One of the main differences between a vocational education and an associate (or higher) degree is that you do not need to complete any "general education" classes for a vocational certificate. For example, when students are completing an associate degree, they need to complete course work in the physical and/or biological sciences, social and/or behavioral sciences, arts, humanities, speech, and other subjects. The portion of a degree that covers this wide range of subjects is usually called "general education" or sometimes "liberal studies" or "liberal arts." All students who are completing associate degrees must complete their general education (no matter what they are majoring in), plus course work that focuses on their major. When you complete a vocational certificate or program, *it is like completing just the "major,"* because the general education portion is not usually required for a vocational certificate or program. That is why it is not considered a "college degree," but rather a certificate.

Associate Degrees

Some careers require you to have specific preparation in your field as well as a foundation of general education. You meet these requirements by earning an associate degree. This type of degree provides you with a broad education (usually referred to as "general education") in the areas of science (physical and/or biological), mathematics, social and behavioral science, arts and humanities, and English, as well as the opportunity to concentrate your studies in a specific area, which is referred to as a "major." Associate degrees are offered through community colleges.

You can complete an associate degree on its own, complete the degree and transfer to a four-year university to continue your education, or transfer to the four-year university without ever completing the associate degree. Depending on the availability of classes and the choices you make, it is reasonable to complete an associate degree in about two years.

Some of the careers that an associate degree will prepare you for are as follows:

- Electrical technician
- Actor
- Public relations specialist
- Sports nutritionist
- Dance teacher
- Athlete
- Public speaker
- Mediator
- Computer systems analyst
- Accountant
- Hospital administrator
- Forester
- Manager (all fields)
- Advertising specialist
- Writer
- Fund-raiser

It's a good idea to get an associate degree if you think you might need to start working as soon as possible after school and may not begin working on a bachelor's degree immediately. Some employers regard an associate degree as the minimum educational requirement rather than a high school diploma. It depends on the field you are going into. Also, in some professions you may need the associate degree to enter the field, but once you're in the field, gaining experience may be more important than an additional academic degree. In both cases, it makes sense to get an associate degree.

You can usually earn an associate degree while you are already working, because most community colleges offer day and evening classes. However, if you are working while you are going to school, you will need to be very careful about only taking on a course load that you can handle and not overloading yourself. This is doubly true if you have small children. Remember that for every hour you spend in class, you are expected to spend one to two hours studying or doing other class work (e.g., writing papers, meeting with tutors, or other activities) outside of class.

When I was a community college student, I worked full-time during the day and took classes at night. I found that when I took one class a semester, I got an A. If I took two classes in a semester, I would get either two B's or an A and a B. If I tried to take three classes, I had to work very, very hard for B's and C's. You see where this is going! *Do yourself a favor, and set yourself up for success by building a schedule that is as realistic and manageable as possible.*

When you think about working on your college degree, you may feel a little panicky. If you've been out of school for a while, you may feel like you are behind in your education and put pressure on yourself to finish quickly. I am going to suggest to you that you *change your focus from finishing quickly to finishing well.* Here's why. Your grade point average (GPA) is *very important.* It's like an academic credit rating. You need to keep it high if you want to apply to four-year schools or graduate schools, especially if your major is very competitive. If you overload yourself in the hopes of getting done faster, you may struggle to keep up and your GPA could suffer. I've seen this happen over and over. Do yourself a big favor and choose finishing well over finishing fast.

Here are two smart rules for success in college (so you can save yourself time, money, and energy and get on with your career):

1. **Take only classes that you need**. Meet with a counselor to get a degree plan that shows you which classes you need to take. Don't take anything that isn't on your degree plan. If you aren't sure if something counts toward your degree, ask a counselor.
2. **Pass every class that you take**. Don't drop classes unless there is absolutely no other option available to you. Many students

don't know that if you drop the class too late in the semester, the instructor will usually have to give you whatever grade you were earning *at the time you dropped*. If you aren't doing well and you are desperate, talk to your instructor. See what you would need to do to get a C and *do it*. Drop the class only if it would be absolutely impossible for you to earn a passing grade.

A note about transferring to four-year universities:

Many students ask me if the major they choose for their associate degree has to be *exactly the same* as the major they are choosing for their bachelor's degree down the road. For example, a student may ask, "Can I major in accounting for my associate degree if I'm planning to transfer into the business administration major for my bachelor's degree?" The answer to this question is that the four-year university really does not care what your major was for your associate degree. *What they really care about is that you have completed all of the course work and other requirements to transfer into the major at their college.* So for the student in this example, if being an accounting major for the associate degree lets him or her complete the four-year university's transfer requirements to go into the business administration bachelor's degree program, then great! If he or she could complete those requirements with a marketing, economics, or management major for the associate degree, any one of those would be fine too. *The name of the major is not important; meeting the transfer requirements is.*

Of course there may be exceptions to this, and transfer requirements change regularly, so definitely speak to a counselor at your college for the most up-to-date information for the college system in your state.

Bachelor's Degrees

When people refer to a college education, they are usually thinking of a bachelor's degree. These degrees are offered at universities (not community colleges) and usually take close to four years to complete. If you complete your first two years of general education courses at a community college, you can transfer to a university as a junior and focus on the courses in your chosen field of study (i.e., major) at the university. Bachelor's degrees are offered through public universities and private universities. There are a number of online bachelor's degree programs as well.

You usually complete a bachelor's degree through the combination of the following:

- Completing "general education" courses
- Completing "major" courses (courses you complete for your specific area of study)
- Meeting the minimum amount of required units for your degree
- Having the necessary GPA to graduate from your university
- Completing any other requirements the university has; for example, being in "good standing"

Some of the careers that a bachelor's degree prepare you for are as follows:

- Public administrator
- TV news broadcaster
- Art advisor
- Journalist
- Advertising specialist
- Clergy
- Training specialist

- Employment interviewer
- Artist
- Writer
- Journalist
- Musician
- Medical and scientific illustrator

Please note that these career lists represent a very small portion of the jobs that these levels of education will prepare you for. As you continue with your research, you will find that there are many more career options at each education level.

If you are thinking about completing a bachelor's degree program online, you may wonder about the reputations of certain online programs. After all, you would be putting your time, energy, and money into a bachelor's degree program even if it's online; you would want to know that your investment would be worthwhile. One of the best ways to find out about the reputation of a program is to check with other people in your field of interest and find out if they've heard of the program you're considering. If they have, ask them what they think of it or how they think it is regarded in the field. Do they know or work with anyone who is a graduate of that particular bachelor's degree program? If the feedback is negative, ask which other programs have a better reputation.

If you are interested in completing a bachelor's degree, I would highly recommend that you begin your education in a community college and then transfer to a four-year university for your bachelor's degree. There are a few very good reasons for this:

1. **You will pay less money for your first two years (lower division) of general education and lower-division major preparation**. If you choose transferrable classes that are equivalent to the ones you need at the four-year university,

you will get the same college credit for sometimes one-fourth of the tuition costs. Yes, you read that right. *The same college credit for lower cost.* Work with a counselor to make sure you are choosing your classes correctly to fulfill your lower-division requirements for transfer.

2. **Since you will be paying less money for your classes, you will be able to invest in a career guidance class.** This will help you determine a career direction and then make smart choices about the college courses you need to get there. You can avoid a situation where you discover you are in the wrong major for your career or are pursuing a field that doesn't actually align with your strengths and values.

3. **Faculty at most community colleges must have a master's degree (or the equivalent) to teach classes.** At many four-year universities, large lecture classes are taught by teaching assistants who do not have master's degrees, because the "professor of record" (i.e., the official teacher) is conducting research. This means that you often have access to higher-quality instruction in a community college.

4. **Many community college class sizes are smaller than university class sizes.** This allows you to have more access to community college instructors.

5. **Students who transfer from community colleges are just as successful in completing their education as students who start out at the four-year university.** When the American Association of Community Colleges published their October 2012 Policy Brief (http://www.aacc.nche.edu/Publications/Briefs/Documents/AACC_Transfer_to_LUMINA.pdf), they reported that students who transferred to four-year universities from community colleges were as successful as students who began their college studies at the four-year university.

Getting Experience

Getting Experience

Getting experience in the fields you are interested in is the best way to prepare yourself for your career, because it will allow you to make an educated choice about your ultimate career goal and do some valuable networking along the way. The contacts you make are valuable resources that can keep you informed about developments in the field and possible upcoming opportunities. Having experience in a field makes you a much more attractive candidate than someone who does not have experience. Many times, if there are two candidates for a position and both have the same skills and the same amount of education, the job offer will go to the candidate with the most experience.

You may find that as you become more familiar with the day-to-day tasks involved in your chosen career, you do not find it as interesting or satisfying as you thought you would. That's all right, because that is a normal part of the process of choosing a career. If you discover during your career preparations that a certain career is not right for you after all, give some very serious thought to your options. You may be able to find a "career niche," a specialized area within a particular field, that is a better fit for you. Make an appointment with a career counselor at a community college to discuss your options.

Many people find that it is difficult to get a job in their chosen field without prior experience. Essentially, they need experience to get the job, but they need the job to get the experience. Talk about frustrating! Luckily, there are some ways to work around that challenge. Pathways around that obstacle include internships, volunteer opportunities, and apprenticeships.

Internships

Let me let you in on another secret: *the job you are learning about in the classroom will look different once you actually start doing it.* Maybe it won't be completely different, but there will definitely be things that you didn't think you would be doing. Hopefully, some of these unexpected parts of your real job will be happy surprises. Unfortunately, some of them will not. For example, I was very excited about the idea of helping elementary school students as an elementary school counselor, until I discovered through my internship that many of the children I was working with were being sent to counseling against their will because of disciplinary issues. Many of them hated having to go to counseling and saw it as punishment. Another challenge I did not foresee was how many parents are not able or willing to give their children a loving environment. Although these discoveries were disappointing for me, they helped guide my decision to work with adults. When I learned that vital difference between what I was learning in my counseling education and what I would actually be doing as a counselor, I was able to shift toward working with college students, which is a much better fit for me. The point is that I absolutely needed that additional real-world perspective provided by the internship experience to make a choice that was a good match.

Internships offer valuable experience and help you do some very important things. First, internships help you decide whether the career you've chosen is actually a good fit for you and if you will be happy in it. Second, internships provide you with work-related experience, which you can then use on your resume when you apply for positions. Third, internships connect you to contacts in your field that can help you get jobs.

There are basically two types of internships: paid and unpaid. Paid internships generally require that you have completed some of your career-related education and developed some of the necessary skills to perform the job you want. Unpaid internships usually have less-strict requirements and are useful entry-level positions to learn skills on the job.

See if there are any books that describe how to intern successfully in your field. You can find important information about what would be expected of you and what you can expect on-site.

A word of caution: whether your internship is paid or unpaid, conduct yourself with the utmost professionalism during your internship. You are establishing a reputation for yourself. You would be surprised how tenacious a bad reputation can be, even in a larger profession, and in a smaller field it can prevent you from receiving any opportunities at all. Understand what is expected of you and be professional. You will be asking for a letter of recommendation so that you can benefit from all of your hard work (see "Letters of Recommendation" at the end of the chapter). *Many internships lead to opportunities for paid positions within the organization.*

The Bureau of Labor Statistics offers additional information about how you can benefit from internships. For a great article about how you can benefit from an internship and how to apply for one, Google Elka Jones's article in the *Occupational Outlook Quarterly* (Summer 2006), "Internships: Previewing a Profession."

Volunteer Opportunities

Volunteer opportunities are similar to unpaid internships, but they are generally less structured. Many people make the mistake of assuming that since they aren't being paid to volunteer, it is okay to behave in ways they would not if they were being paid. For example, you may be the type of employee who is always punctual, but you may believe it is okay to be a little late when you are volunteering, because, after all, you are "working for free." To get the most out of your volunteer opportunity, it is a good idea to behave as though you are being paid.

When you volunteer for an organization, you are developing a reputation just as you would if you were a paid employee. The people whom you work with will remember that they could depend on you, that you took the initiative to get things done, and that you were willing to cooperate with your coworkers.

Just as with internships, volunteer opportunities allow you to learn about your chosen field and to develop valuable experience to make you an attractive and competitive candidate for a position. Your professionalism could turn today's volunteer position into tomorrow's paying job!

To find volunteer opportunities, contact professional organizations in your career field. You can also find volunteer opportunities via websites like www.volunteermatch.org and www.idealist.org.

Apprenticeships

Apprenticeships are available in many different fields, including construction, manufacturing, telecommunications, environmental protection, culinary arts, health care, child care, and the arts (Crosby,

2002). They are generally a combination of on-the-job experience and classroom instruction.

According to Olivia Crosby's article in the *Occupational Outlook Quarterly* (Summer 2002), any occupation can be registered as apprenticable as long as it meets four criteria:

- It is clearly defined.
- It is customarily learned on the job.
- It requires manual, mechanical, or technical skill.
- It requires at least 2,000 hours of work experience and, usually, at least 144 hours of related instruction.

The Bureau of Labor Statistics regularly publishes information about apprenticeships, such as which occupations are suitable and how to get information about a particular apprenticeship program.

Letters of Recommendation

Toward the end of your internship, volunteer opportunity, or apprenticeship, you ask for letters of recommendation so that you can highlight all of the experience you have gained when you are applying for paying opportunities in your field. Ask for letters of recommendation from the people you have worked with directly who have the most in-depth knowledge of your professionalism, knowledge, and skills. These would usually include your boss or direct supervisor. A lot of people make the mistake of asking for letters of recommendation from people who don't really know anything specific about the person asking. Sometimes this is because the person who is asking for the letter of recommendation is asking the wrong person. For example, if you worked regularly with your boss, but instead of asking her for a letter of recommendation you ask *her boss* (because you think the *boss's boss's* recommendation would carry more weight), you aren't likely to get that letter. It isn't personal. They just don't really know enough about you to write it.

Other times, the person asking hasn't really done anything special to stand out, so the letter writer doesn't have anything special to write about him or her. Don't let that person be you. Do your best work and make sure to let any potential writers know when you receive positive feedback about your work from others. For your professionalism and hard work to pay off in glowing letters from your supervisors and colleagues describing your accomplishments and assets, they need to know what those accomplishments are.

When you ask for a letter of recommendation or anything else from someone that is requiring them to do work for you for free, make it easy. Be considerate of the writer. If you need the letter by a particular date, give the writer three to four weeks to write your letter. Give the writer any information he or she can use to make the letter more specific. For example, you may give the writer a list of your accomplishments on the job or include a copy of your transcripts to show them the grades you have earned. If your letter is going to a specific institution, include the name and address of the institution so that it can be included in the header. Last, if you are requesting that the letter be mailed directly to a particular organization, include an addressed and stamped envelope with your request for the letter. If you do request that the letter be sent to a specific institution, ask for a copy to keep for your files.

In addition to the career boost you get from receiving letters of recommendation, it is personally gratifying to read positive observations about your work performance, and it reminds you how much you have to offer your profession. When you are working hard and things are difficult, it can feel really good to take a look at those letters and remind yourself that others see your strengths and positive qualities!

Your Resume

Resumes

A good resume will get you an interview. A bad resume might not be looked at twice. Before we go into detail about writing resumes, here are some important things to keep in mind:

- **Be concise.** When you are writing your resume, think of clear, concise ways to list your skills and experience. Try not to be too wordy or vague. If your resume is not clear about how your skills apply to the job opening, potential employers may assume you are not qualified for the position.
- **Know your audience.** Do some research about the companies you are applying to so you can customize your "career objective" statement for each company.
- **Use an appropriate font.** Don't try to personalize your resume with an unusual font. You want potential employers to remember your resume because of its professional appearance, not because it had a fancy, unique font that was difficult to read. Use a clear, common font that is easy to read.

  - Example #1: This font is too hard to read for a resume.
  - Example #2: This font is clear and easy to read.

- **Present yourself professionally**. Use good-quality paper to print your resume and cover letter. You can purchase resume paper at most office supply stores like Staples and Office Depot. Although most often you will be submitting your resume electronically, *you will be expected to bring in printed resumes for interviews*, so be prepared.
- **Be thorough**. Include a cover letter. Answer all questions asked in the application. Proofread and have someone else proofread it for spelling and grammatical errors.

Now we will go into more detail about types of resumes, how to write resumes, and resources you can use to get help with your resume.

Writing Your Resume

The first thing to do when creating your resume is to collect all the important facts so that you have them at your fingertips. For example, some information that you may not have off the top of your head might include addresses for your previous job sites, dates of previous employment, job titles, and phone numbers of references.

It is *absolutely essential* for you to include the following information in your resume:

- Name
- Address
- Phone number
- Work experience
- Education
- References

Your name, address, and phone number will be a part of your "heading." Your work experience will be a separate section, as will your education and references.

Depending on your employment background, educational background, and the type of job you are applying for, you may also want to include information about the following. Each of these will be a separate section:

- Job objective
- Honors
- Special skills
- Publications
- Professional memberships
- Activities (relevant to job)
- Certificates and licenses

Once you have the information you want to include gathered together, you will need to choose which type of resume you will create. There are two main types—chronological and functional. They both use the same information, but they organize it in different ways depending on what you want to emphasize about yourself.

Chronological:

All of your work experience is organized chronologically (by date). In a reverse chronological resume, you list your most recent job first and go backward.

The reverse chronological format is good to use if you want to emphasize how your most recent work experience qualifies you for the job you are applying for.

Functional:

In a functional resume you list your work-related accomplishments and achievements near the top of your resume and then the details of your positions (employer address, dates of employment, title of position) further on in the resume.

The functional format is good to use if you have been out of the workforce for a while and/or want to emphasize your specific achievements rather than your general work history.

Take a look at the following templates to familiarize yourself with the differences between the chronological resume format and the functional resume format.

Functional Resume Template
Name
Street – City, State – Zip – Phone – Email

Job Objective
Very concisely state the type of job you would like next. For example you might say, "To contribute to the profitability of a socially responsible company by using my talents and skills in customer service."

Highlights of Qualifications
- Write three or four bullet statements that summarize what you have to contribute that would make you a good candidate. Each statement should be two sentences or less.
- Your statements should highlight your experience, skills, community service, and personality traits that would be relevant for the job.
- Prioritize this section so that the most relevant information comes first.

Professional Accomplishments
Key Skill
- Write two or more bullet statements about employment or volunteer activities in which you used this skill.
- Describe how you impacted the organization, your boss, or your coworkers positively. For example, you might say "Increased sales by 50% over a two year period" or "contributed to success of department by creating a job manual for my position."
- Mention any awards or special recognition you received that used this key skill.
- If you used this key skill to solve problems, briefly describe the problems and your positive results.

Key Skill
- Follow the guidance given in the first section.
- Prioritize the statements under both "Key Skill" areas so the most important information comes first.

Work History (or Volunteer History)
20XX-Present	Organization, City, State (list most current position first)
	Job Title
Date-Date	Organization, City, State (2nd most current position)
	Job Title
Date-Date	Organization, City, State (3rd most current position)
	Job Title

Education
Degree, Major, Graduation Year
School, City, State

Community Service
Position held, Organization, Dates
Position held, Organization, Dates

Excellent references available upon request.

Chronological Resume Template

Name

Street – City, State – Zip – Phone – Email

Job Objective

Very concisely state the type of job you would like next. For example you might say, "To contribute to the profitability of a socially responsible company by using my talents and skills in customer service."

Highlights of Qualifications

- Write three or four bullet statements that summarize what you have to contribute that would make you a good candidate. Each statement should be two sentences or less.
- Your statements should highlight your experience, skills, community service, and personality traits that would be relevant for the job.
- Prioritize this section so that the most relevant information comes first.

ORGANIZATION, City, State, 20XX-Present (List most current position first.)
Job Title

- Write two or more bullet statements about the work you performed at this job and what you learned or accomplished that is relevant to your job objective.
- Describe how you impacted the organization, your boss, or your coworkers positively. For example, you might say "Increased sales by 50% over a two year period" or "contributed to success of department by creating a job manual for my position."
- Mention any awards or special recognition you received while in this position that relate to your job objective.

ORGANIZATION, City, State, Date-Date (List second most current position next.)
Job Title

- Write two or more bullet statements about the work you performed at this job and what you learned or accomplished that is relevant to your job objective.
- Describe how you impacted the organization, your boss, or your coworkers positively. For example, you might say "Increased sales by 50% over a two year period" or "contributed to success of department by creating a job manual for my position."
- Mention any awards or special recognition you received while in this position that relate to your job objective.

ORGANIZATION, City, State, Date-Date (List third most current position next.)
Job Title

- Write two or more bullet statements about the work you performed at this job and what you learned or accomplished that is relevant to your job objective.
- Describe how you impacted the organization, your boss, or your coworkers positively. For example, you might say "Increased sales by 50% over a two year period" or "contributed to success of department by creating a job manual for my position."
- Mention any awards or special recognition you received while in this position that relate to your job objective.

Education

Degree, Major, Graduation Year
School, City, State

Community Service

Position held, Organization, Dates
Position held, Organization, Dates

Excellent references available upon request.

Resume Help

If this is the first time you have written a resume, you may want to get more help. Workshops, career resource websites, books, professional resume writers, and career centers are helpful resources.

Workshops

Workshops are a very good way to get help with your resume. When you attend a resume-writing workshop, you have the benefit of having your questions answered on the spot. Also, workshop facilitators have many other resources that they can refer you to if you need more help than they can provide. Colleges offer resume workshops through their job placement centers, career centers, or career counseling classes. Community centers also offer resume workshops to interested community members.

Websites

Websites that post job opportunities often have tips on writing your resume and avoiding common mistakes. A few good websites to try follow:

www.monster.com
www.careerbuilder.com
www.resume.com

These websites have good advice on creating your resume and allow you to post your resume so prospective employers can find you, but don't count on employers finding you. No matter how good your skills are, you still need to get out there in front of them. Marie Forleo, entrepreneur extraordinaire, says that even if you have the cure for cancer, it's *your* responsibility to learn as much as you can about getting it out there in front of everyone so that they can benefit from it. So get your talented self out there!

Books

If you need more in-depth assistance with your resume or want to see more sample resumes, you may want to get a book on resume writing. Before you spend money to buy a book, see what your local library has to offer. Here are a few books on resume writing to get you started:

- *The Resume.Com Guide to Writing Unbeatable Resumes* by Warren Simmons and Rose Curtis
- *101 Best Resumes: Endorsed by the Professional Association of Resume Writers* by Jay A. Block and Michael Betrus
- *The Resume Handbook: How to Write Outstanding Resumes and Cover Letters for Every Situation (Resume Handbook)* by Arthur D. Rosenberg

Professional Resume Writers

You can also have your resume written for you by a professional. If that is something you would like to do, visit a local career center and get some recommendations for professional resume writers in your area. Once you have the names of some professional resume writers, see if you can contact some of their clients or read their testimonials. If they are not willing to put you in contact with any of their clients or they have no testimonials, you should pass. Also, if you are looking for a professional resume writer or writing service online, definitely check out their websites, but remember that anyone can advertise on the Internet regardless of his or her actual qualifications. If you are at all unsure, it's wise to check prospective resume writers out with the Better Business Bureau before you finalize your choice.

Career Centers

Career centers at colleges are good places to get resume help. In addition to having a variety of resume writing books on hand, there is also usually a staff member who can assist you with tips on organizing your resume. Career centers also usually have a variety of sample resumes for you to look at if you need resume ideas.

Your Cover Letter

Cover Letters

Anytime you send an employer your resume, you should include a cover letter.

The cover letter is important because it

- Introduces you to the company
- Gives the potential employer some background information about your relevant skills and experience
- Describes why you would be a good fit for the position and for the organization.

When you write your cover letter, you will want to keep in mind the following question:

What does this employer need to know about me that will show him or her that I am a good match for this position?

The cover letter has a special structure. It begins with your name, address, phone number, and e-mail address. You will also include the date and the name and address of the person you are sending it to.

- Special note about e-mail addresses—if your regular e-mail address does not sound professional, create a new account for yourself with a professional-sounding e-mail address and use it for your cover letters, resumes, and other job search correspondence. For example, Bob Smith might not want to use his crazybob@domain.com e-mail address. He would be better off creating a new e-mail address with his first initial and last name. It is easy and free to sign up for a new Google e-mail address at www.gmail.com.

The next part of your cover letter is the salutation and the body. Try to find out the name of the person to whom you are sending the resume so that you can address your cover letter to him or her. Otherwise, you may use the salutation "To Whom It May Concern:"

In the body of your cover letter, introduce yourself and tell the reader which job you are interested in. If someone referred you, mention that person. Describe why you are a good candidate for the job and why you would like to work for the company. Let the employer know how best to contact you. Finish the letter with "Sincerely," followed by your name. Don't forget to sign your name in ink. Your cover letter should be about one page long.

Cover Letter Dos and Don'ts

Do:

- Follow the structure for your cover letter.
- Create a professional-looking e-mail address to use if you don't have one. You can create a new Gmail address for free on Google.
- Print your cover letter on the same good-quality paper that you print your resume on.

- Proofread for grammatical, punctuation, and spelling errors.
- Customize your cover letter for each company you apply to.

Don't:

- Don't use the same cover letter for every position you apply for. Instead, try to customize it a little for each position to show that you have done some research on the company you are applying to.
- Don't assume it is okay to leave important information out of the cover letter if it is in your resume. If your cover letter doesn't mention it, the employer may assume you don't have the necessary qualifications or experience and never get to your resume.
- Don't skip the cover letter.

If you do a search online, you can find cover letter templates, advice, and other resources. Here's a sample cover letter to get you started. Each section explains what you need to include.

Your Name
Your Mailing Address
Your City, State and Zip
Your Phone Number
Your Email Address

Today's Date

Your Addressee's Name*
Professional Title
Name of Organization
Mailing Address
City, State and Zip

Dear Mr. or Mrs. Addressee's Last Name,**

Start your letter with a statement that catches your reader's attention and establishes a connection with your reader. For example, you may say, "I am an enthusiastic supporter of your company's mission and I am excited about the opportunity to use my skills to support it." You should also briefly mention which job you are applying for.

Briefly describe why you would be a good applicant for the position. It's a good idea to review the description in the advertisement for the position and address how you fit each of the qualifications. This method gives you a structure to work with and ensures that you do not forget to mention your relevant skills. If it helps make your cover letter clearer and more concise, you can use a bullet point format here.

Close by thanking the reader for taking the time to read your cover letter and expressing your interest in hearing from them. You could say something like, "I appreciate your consideration and look forward to hearing from you if the attached resume indicates that I am a good fit for the position. Thank you for your time."

Sincerely,

(Your Signature)
Your Name Typed

Encl: Resume

*If you do not know the addressee's name, you may leave this blank however you must address it to a specific job title or department, for example "Director of Personnel" or "Human Resources."
**If you do not know the addressee's name, you may use "To Whom It May Concern," in its place.

Cover Letter Help

Books:

- *Cover Letter Magic: Trade Secrets of Professional Resume Writers* by Wendy S. Enelow and Louise Kursmark
- *No-Nonsense Cover Letters: The Essential Guide to Creating Attention-Grabbing Cover Letters That Get Interviews and Job Offers* by Wendy S. Enelow and Arnold G. Boldt

Websites:

About.com: cover letter tips and samples
http://jobsearch.about.com/od/coverletterwriting/Cover_Letter_Writing.htm

QuintCareers.com: professional cover letter samples
http://www.quintcareers.com/cover_letter_samples.html

Resume-Help.org: resume tips, cover letter writing tips, etc.
http://www.resume-help.org/cover_letter_tips.htm

Resumes.Com: resume tips, sample resumes
www.resumes.com

Your Job Search

Where Do You Look for a Job?

When you are finished with your resume and have put together a basic cover letter, you are ready to start your job search. There are a few different ways to find jobs.

- **Postings on job search websites**: Popular job search websites like www.monster.com and www.careerbuilder.com have employment opportunities posted on their websites. Usually you can get more information from a website posting than you can get from a printed classified ad.
- **Career fairs**: Career fairs are another useful resource. Many colleges host career fairs so that local employers have an opportunity to connect to students who are almost ready to graduate. If you are a college student at a college that hosts career fairs, it is definitely worth your time to check it out (even if it's on a day you wouldn't normally be on campus). I know of many people who received job offers through career fairs before they had even completed their degrees! Once they were done, they had jobs to go to right out of college. Make sure you dress exactly as you would for an actual interview and bring copies of your resume. You should also prepare a generic version of your cover letter addressed "To Whom It May Concern."

- **Career centers**: Career centers usually have a bulletin board with job opportunities posted. College career centers often have internships (paid and unpaid) that allow you to get more experience in a field that does not generally offer entry-level positions.

- **Employment or staffing agencies**: Employment agencies help you with your resume, coach you on how to do well in your interviews, and match you with job opportunities that fit your skill level. They serve as a go-between for you and the employer. Once you interview with the employer and you are chosen for the position, the employment agency makes their money by charging the employer a fee for your services. In essence, you work *for* the employment agency, but you work *at* the employer's site. You get a job, the employer (site) gets a qualified employee without having to search for one, and the agency gets a fee for their services. A lot of employees gain access to permanent positions in a company by being placed by an employment agency and then being offered a permanent position by the employment site.

- **Classified ads in newspapers**: Many people find employment opportunities in the classified section of the newspaper. One drawback of responding to a classified ad is the ad does not usually tell you much about the company, so you will have to do some research on your own.

- **Contacting companies directly**: If there are certain companies that you are interested in working for, do some research on their websites about what they do and what positions they are advertising to fill. Find out who is in charge of hiring and send that person your resume and cover letter. You can also go to the company in person to drop off your resume and cover letter. If you go to the company in person, keep in mind that you should dress as professionally as you would if you were coming in for an interview. In other words, wear a business suit. Bring the information you need to complete an application in case you will be filling out an application at the company. *Don't* *forget to bring a pen.* I have heard of companies providing red pens for applicants who have not brought their own as a way to flag the applications of unprepared applicants. The red ink on the application lets them know the applicant wasn't prepared.

- **Networking**: Getting to know people in the field you want to work in is a great way to find out about job opportunities. You may already know people who are doing what you would like to do. Give them a call and see if they would be willing to give you some pointers about getting into the field over a cup of coffee (your treat). Another great way to get to know people in the field is to join professional organizations in the field you are interested in. Membership fees for students are generally lower than membership fees for professionals already working in the field. Many professional organizations host conferences for their members to update them on developments in the field and give them the opportunity to network. Always remember that networking is a two-way street. When you ask a favor of someone, it is considered common courtesy to return the favor. When you network, you are creating your reputation, so behave professionally (e.g., be on time, dress for work, etc.). Do not take your contacts (i.e., people you know) for granted or get in the habit of looking at people only in terms of what they can offer you. Ask, but don't take it for granted that everyone you would like to receive professional advice from is willing to provide it for free. Professional consultants make their living providing advice. You would not ask a doctor to take out your tonsils for free, because you know their time is valuable. Be respectful of a consultant's time as well.

Social Media and the Internet

Using the Internet to search for job opportunities is the most popular way of finding job openings. Sites such as www.monster.com and www.

jobs.com are widely used sites that give information about openings as well as career-related information. They are easy to use and navigate.

Keep in mind that just as you are able to use the Internet to find out information about potential openings, your potential employers are able to use it to find out information about you. If you are in the habit of posting your pictures on sites like Facebook, do so judiciously. Learn about and take advantage of the privacy options on Facebook and other similar sites, so that you can control the information people can access about you and the pictures of you they can see. Don't be too eager to "tag" yourself or confirm others' requests to tag you in pictures that don't present you in a positive light. An occasion when you are dancing with an attractive person with a drink in your hand at a party could be a moment that you would like to remember and share with your friends, but it could give a potential employer the impression that you are irresponsible or even an alcoholic. Unfair? Yes. True? Definitely. Remember that although the Internet connects us in fantastic ways that never were available before, this also means that whatever image of yourself you choose to present can be shared far and wide and in some cases cannot be removed from the Internet.

Another mistake people often make is not realizing whom they are connected to in terms of Facebook friends. A common scenario is that people complain about their job in general and the coworkers with whom they are Facebook "friends" see the complaint. Sometimes the person who sees the complaint is the complainer's boss. Either scenario can result in the person who complained being fired.

Contacting the Employer

Once you have located a job opportunity, you will need to contact the company. If you find the opportunity through a classified ad or Internet posting, you will find that instructions on contacting the company are included in the ad. Occasionally a potential employer will contact you after seeing your resume posted on a job search website, but again, do not count on others seeking you out. Take the initiative.

If you find the opportunity through a networking contact, your contact will generally tell you whom you should contact at the company. If you are unsure whom to contact, it is always best to contact the human resources department of the company. The human resources department is usually in charge of hiring and screening applicants. They will generally request that you send your resume and cover letter to the company to the attention of the human resources division.

This is when all of the hard work you put in to writing a professional, good-looking resume and cover letter pays off!

Sometimes additional materials besides a resume are required to apply for the job you are interested in. You may have to fill in an application. You may need to provide paperwork to prove you hold required certification for the job you are applying for. You may need to confirm your level of education by providing official transcripts that show the degree you earned. You may need to answer "supplemental questions" as a part of the application process. Whatever the situation, make sure you are thorough and provide all of the information requested. Leaving an important piece out may remove you from consideration. A busy employer may not have time to contact you to ask for the missing information again or may assume you are forgetful or careless… not the impression that you want to leave.

Be respectful toward everyone, period. Keep in mind that you are creating a reputation for yourself from the moment of your first point of contact with the company. Be polite and professional with *everyone you speak to, but especially administrative assistants (i.e., secretaries, office managers, etc.).* Administrative assistants influence the person you may be interviewing with or working for. Busy people often trust the opinions of their administrative assistants. Treat everyone you encounter with respect, even if you don't think you'll have any future contact with them at all.

I was once treated in an extremely disrespectful manner by a person I was interviewing, because she thought I worked for the interviewer. She didn't realize that I *was* one of the interviewers! The candidate met with my colleague at first. While my colleague was present, the candidate was friendly and answered his questions in a very open and professional manner. When my colleague introduced me to the candidate and left, I began asking the candidate the interview questions. As soon as my colleague left and we were alone, her manner changed abruptly. Her friendliness evaporated, her tone went from helpful to annoyed, and she flat out *refused to answer any of my questions.* She further expressed her impatience with me by sighing, loudly and repeatedly, and checking her watch. I decided to end the interview and walked her to the door. I offered to shake hand, and she refused to touch my hand. As she walked out, she turned and disdainfully said, "You can let *them* know upstairs that I am qualified for this position."

I replied, "Actually, I will be one of the people making that decision." Once she understood her mistake (the look on her face was truly priceless), she tried to make up for her rudeness, but by then she had already created an extremely unflattering impression of herself. Needless to say, she was not offered the position. No one is impressed by arrogance. Be nice to everyone.

Following Up

Once you have submitted your resume, cover letter, and any other application materials, you will want to follow up with the potential employer to make sure they have received your materials. A week after you send the materials, contact human resources to make sure they have been received.

Most companies will give you a date by which they plan to contact applicants for interviews. If you have not heard anything by that date, contact the human resources department to see what the status of your application is. *Do not contact the company to check your application status before the date they gave.* No matter how eager you are to hear back, *do not call before the deadline.* The human resources department may have several pending openings to screen applicants for, and the staff will not appreciate having to divert time and effort away from the ones with earlier deadlines.

There are many reasons applicants *do not* receive an interview:

- **The applicant's qualifications are not right for the job** (e.g., not enough experience, applicant does not hold appropriate credential or degree, applicant does not have necessary skills).
- **The application form was not filled out completely.**
- **Important requested documentation was not included in the application packet sent to the company.**
- **The field is highly competitive.** When there are large numbers of applicants and few openings, employers interview a smaller percentage of applicants than they would otherwise.

Tip—The best way to combat this is to make yourself a more competitive candidate by gaining experience through internships, developing necessary skills, and getting additional education.

If your qualifications are right for the job, you will most likely be contacted to schedule an interview.

Interviews

Interviewing

The secret to doing well in your interview is simple: *be prepared.*

The basics of preparing for your interview are as follows:

- **Do some research on the company.**
- **Anticipate the kinds of questions you may be asked and practice how you will respond to them.**
- **Prepare for the practical details.**

Let's go into a little more detail about each of these things.

Researching the Company

Websites are a job applicant's best friend. Find out if they have any new products, projects, or partnerships that they are excited about. When you mention these things during an interview, you will be perceived as informed and enthusiastic. At the end of the interview, you will usually be asked if you have any questions for the interviewer. If you have done research on the company, you will be prepared to ask an intelligent, informed question about the company's productivity, mission, goals, etc.

Anticipating and Responding to Questions

It is possible to prepare for the majority of the questions you will be asked, because many interview questions are similar in every interview and in every field of employment. In addition to questions about your specific experience, education, goals, knowledge of the industry, and how those things can benefit your potential employer, you will probably be asked some or all of the following commonly asked questions. Here are some such questions, an explanation of what the questions really mean, and some examples of responses. Remember that it's okay to be a little nervous. If your interviewer notices that you are nervous, you can simply admit that you are a bit nervous because you are very excited about the opportunity. He or she will appreciate knowing that you are taking the experience seriously because the opportunity is important to you.

Commonly Asked Interview Question #1—
What are your strengths and weaknesses?

Sometimes this question is broken down into two separate questions—one about your strengths and one about your weaknesses. You will want to talk about your strengths *as they relate to the job.* The "weakness" question is a little trickier. A good rule of thumb is to avoid stating your actual weaknesses. Sounds weird, right? Here's what you do instead. Talk about *how you have overcome a challenging behavior in the past.* When you do this, be as honest as possible while still presenting yourself as a responsible person who can work with others.

Wrong Response—
"Being a good athlete is one of my strengths—my abs are ripped! One of my weaknesses is that I am always late."

Better Response—

"My experience as an athlete has taught me to be a *good team player* and *focus on achieving positive results for the group*. I used to have a little bit of difficulty staying organized, but now I handle *time management* by using the calendar in my phone to keep track of my schedule."

Commonly Asked Interview Question #2—
Why do you want to work for ABC Company?

Do not misinterpret this question as "Why do you want a job?" The interviewer is trying to find out *what specifically about ABC Company motivated you to choose to apply there.* If you have specific information about the company that you can include in your response, include it. This is where your research on their website pays off, because if you've done your research, you will instantly set yourself apart from the other candidates. It's so easy to take twenty minutes and do a bit of research about the company you want to work at, and it makes such a strong positive impression that you will wonder why more people don't do it. While it's great to use your research to dazzle your potential employer, it's also valuable for your own decision making. Your research on the company should help you decide if it is truly a place where you would like to work.

Wrong Response—

"I really need a job, and a friend of mine said you were hiring."

Better Response—

"During my job search, I researched several companies. I learned that ABC Company has a good reputation in the industry for (fill in the blank). When I found out there were employment opportunities at ABC Company, I felt my education and experience would be a good match for the position."

Commonly Asked Interview Question #3—
Why did you leave your last job?

Even if you left your last job because your boss was a jerk, this is not the time to complain about him or her. If you bad-mouth your previous boss to prospective bosses, they will assume you will do the same about them. Also, if your previous job was in the same industry, your previous and prospective employers may know each other. They might even be friends!

Wrong Response—
"My last boss was a complete jerk. I would rather work anywhere than work back there."

Better Response—
"I learned a lot in my previous (or current) position and I consistently contributed to the success of the team, but opportunities there are limited and I am ready for a new challenge."

Commonly Asked Interview Question #4—
Where do you see yourself in five years?

The interviewer wants to know two things: do you have long-term goals, and if so, what are they? Novice interviewees sometimes try to impress the interviewer with grand predictions of their future success at the company. Avoid this! Such behavior usually comes across as overconfidence and immaturity. Show that you are realistic and willing to work toward future opportunities for advancement.

Wrong Response—
"In your chair."

Better Response—
"I am willing to work for the opportunity to advance, so it would depend on how my work is perceived, the skills I gain along the way, and the opportunities that will be here for me to grow into."

Commonly Asked Interview Question #5—
What salary are you expecting?

If you are asked this question, it means the salary is negotiable. *The key to negotiation is not to be the first person to give a number.* If your number is too high, they will assume you are overqualified, ill-informed, or unrealistic in your expectations. If your number is too low, they will agree to it immediately and you will be stuck making less than you could have made. It is best to put the ball back in their court and let them give you a number. Then you can decide if it's fair and either accept it or ask for the salary you think is appropriate.

How do you know what a reasonable salary is for the job you're applying for? Job search sites like www.indeed.com and www.glassdoor.com let you search for jobs in your state by title and compare salaries. Get an idea of what other employers are advertising for similar positions, and you will know what is fair to expect in your field.

Wrong Response—
"I can start at whatever your highest-paid employees make that do this job," or "I'll take whatever your entry-level employees start at."

Better Response—
"I would be willing to consider your strongest offer."

Practical Details

In addition to researching the company and preparing to answer questions about your experience and preferred salary, you will have some other practical details to consider, such as the following:

- **Nervousness**: It is very natural to be nervous about your interview. Keep in mind that many people are nervous when interviewing and interviewers generally expect it. Sometimes, mentioning that you are nervous about the interview can help break the ice. A sympathetic interviewer will try to help alleviate your anxiety. The secret weapon to fighting nervousness is preparation. Practice your answers to the common questions. Practice talking about your strengths. Practice describing your experience. Practice, practice, practice!
- **Being worried about sounding "fake"**: The more you practice your responses, the more natural they will be in your interview. Practice is truly the key.
- **Logistics (e.g., where to go, where to park, whom to speak with)**: You may be concerned about finding your way to the interview location. The easiest way to relieve that concern is to plan your route in advance. Use a mapping website like www.mapquest.com for door-to-door directions. If possible, drive the route a few days before to get an idea of where you are going and plan for possible delays (e.g., heavy traffic, road work, detours). Traffic apps like SigAlert.com give you live traffic reports so you can see how long it will really take you to get there.

- **Appropriate attire**: Dressing appropriately for an interview depends on three things: the industry you are interviewing in, the geographic location, and the weather. For example, if you are interning in a recording studio, tattoos may be fine, whereas in a law firm they might not be okay. In some areas of the United States, it is appropriate to wear jeans and blazers to interviews, while in others it wouldn't work. In any case, make sure your clothes are clean and have no wrinkles. If you clothes are washable and you need to get the wrinkles out fast, spray them with a little water and put them in the dryer for five minutes. It will get the wrinkles out. Skip perfume or cologne, because you don't know what scents your potential interviewer may be allergic to or have bad memories of. Many websites and books are available to advise you on appropriate business attire. Take advantage of these resources so that you can walk into your interview feeling confident. Take the safe route for your interview, and when/if you get the job, you can dress more casually if that's okay where you work.

  Do not wear baggy clothing, sexy clothing, overly dressy evening wear (e.g., sequins), sloppy or wrinkled clothing, loungewear, or club wear. Underwear should not be visible— it's called underwear for a reason. No visible bra straps!

- **Necessary documentation:** You may have been asked to provide documentation about your right to work in the United States. You may have been asked to bring in confirmation of certain certifications that are required for the position. Make sure you remember to bring those things with you, preferably in a folder or envelope that keeps them from being tattered or folded. Bring copies of any letters of recommendation, thank you notes for superior work you have done, and positive performance reviews from previous employers. Your interviewers may not ask for them, but they might help you answer questions about your strengths and accomplishments.

- The night before the interview, get your rest. Your brain will do a better job of helping you answer interview questions if you give it some rest. The day of the interview, eat a light breakfast. You want to have energy without your stomach making noise all during your interview.
- If you feel yourself getting nervous the day of the interview, breathe deeply and smile. When you breathe deeply, you tell your body that it can relax. When you smile, you send signals to your brain that it can relax too.
- After your interview, send a thank you card to each of your interviewers if possible. Get their names during the interview or call afterward and ask for their names.

Following Up

After your interview you will hear back from the company. Hopefully, you will receive a job offer.

If you get a job offer—

Make sure you understand the conditions of your employment before accepting the job offer. For example, you will want to confirm the following:

- Your salary
- Your schedule
- Where you will work
- Whom you will report to
- Your benefits package, if available (e.g., health benefits, sick time, vacation time)

This is also a good time to ask any questions that you did not ask during the interview.

If you do not get a job offer—

It is possible that another applicant was simply more experienced than you or had more of the skills necessary to perform the job well. Some interviewers are happy to give you feedback on how you can improve; others see requests for feedback as "pushy." If you decide that it would not benefit you in your situation to request feedback, chalk it up to experience and move ahead to the next opportunity.

Another way that you might get better insight into why you did not receive a job offer is to consider if you were asked questions that you were unable to answer or questions that you did not answer well. Were there areas of experience that you lack? If so, consider building experience through volunteer opportunities. Did the opening require skills that you don't have? Look into classes that will help you get those skills.

Finally, consider the fact that it might just not have been a good match for you. For example, I was once advised during a mock interview to express myself in a manner that was much more "high-energy" to convey my passion to potential interviewers. This approach did not feel authentic to me, and I finally decided that it would be better for me to present my most professional and authentic self instead. If I had accepted a job offer based on an interview in which I pretended to be someone else, I wouldn't have been happy there. Being "fake" is not professionalism. Improving your skills, taking an interest in how you present yourself to the world, and being willing to learn are authentic expressions of yourself; these things help you get where you want to go.

A Few Last Things to Remember

- The more job openings you apply for, the better your chances of receiving an interview. The more interviews you go on, the better your chances of a job offer. Persevere through all of the nos so you can get to your yes. Keep going.
- While you are looking for a job, think of your job search as your temporary job. Take it seriously. Plan your time wisely, and set aside a specific amount of time each day that you devote to your job search activities. Marie Forleo, a multitalented entrepreneur, says, "If it's not on your calendar, it doesn't exist."
- Stay or become involved in the field. Attend conferences, workshops, trade shows, and lectures. Read current publications to inform yourself about trends in the industry you are applying to. You can usually join professional organizations in your field with a "student membership" if you are in school, which gives you access to people you can talk to who are already doing what you want to be doing. As you build relationships with them and they see your interest and abilities, they will keep you in mind for opportunities and positions.
- Consider alternatives. Was there another option you discovered during your job search that interested you? Is there another field that is similar to your first choice that you could apply to? Do you have skills that you hadn't considered? Recognize when it may be time to take a different direction.
- Stay optimistic, and keep your "self-talk" positive. Remind yourself that all of your ongoing preparation is helping you be a competitive candidate for the position you want.
- Take care of yourself. You probably hear this advice often and may ignore it, but taking care of your health is what gives you the stamina and energy to move forward in your life and manage the stress that is created by all of the good changes

you are making. Get enough rest and exercise, eat healthfully, and look to your healthiest relationships for support. Nurture your spirit. Remind yourself that your gifts are needed out in the world.

And finally,

Thank you for letting me share this information with you. I believe that every person has unique gifts and strengths; the world needs yours. Keep learning what you need to know, and stay open to new possibilities along the way. I wish you the best of luck as you create the life that you want and move in the direction of your dreams!

GLOSSARY

Apprenticeship: A way of gaining career experience through a combination of on-the-job skill development and classroom instruction.

Associate degree: A degree offered by a community college that usually includes a combination of completion of a broad range of "general education" courses, a minimum GPA requirement, and a minimum amount of units or credits. The course work can also include some courses in a concentrated area of study or "major." Can be an associate of arts degree (AA) or an associate of science degree (AS).

Bachelor's degree: A degree offered by a public or private university that includes a combination of completion of a broad range of "general education" courses, a minimum GPA requirement, and a minimum amount of units or credits. Must include considerable focus on courses in a concentrated area of study or "major." Can be a bachelor of arts degree (BA) or a bachelor of science degree (BS).

Career niche: A specific area of a profession that requires a specialized skill set and/or a particular type of experience.

GPA: Grade point average. The grade point average is used as a measurement to describe overall academic performance by semester.

It is also used to describe overall academic performance from the beginning of one's postsecondary education to the current semester.

Internship: A way of gaining career experience in a "white-collar" profession. The internship can be paid or unpaid; however, paid internships generally require a more advanced skill set than unpaid internships within the same field.

Letter of recommendation: A letter of recommendation from a past or current supervisor (or instructor) describes how the combination of your skills, experience, education, and/or personality makes you a good candidate for your future opportunities. It can be general or specific.

Major: In academe, a "major" refers to a concentrated area within a particular field of study.

Vocational education: A vocational education program provides "hands-on" experience in a particular field.